DREAM IT PLAN IT
LIVE IT

7/10/2016 .

LEGAL NOTICES

DREAM IT
PLAN IT
LIVE IT

YOUR FINANCIAL LIFE PLAN

Karl Lehmann

Master Creating Your Own Financial Freedom Fund

To gain access to all downloadable resources that have been included in this book please visit:

dreamitplanitliveitbook.com

<u>Special Note:</u> **For a limited time only** – leave your details by following the link below.

dreamitplanitliveitbook.com

TABLE OF CONTENTS

PART THREE:
Review Your Wealth Management
Strategy And Keeping It On Track

ACKNOWLEDGEMENTS

A book written to tackle 'Designing The Life You Want,' rather than merely allowing life to happen, will undoubtedly have had many influencers. I've touched on a few inspiring personalities here, but there are many more whom I've met along the way. I thank you all.

To Dad. You left me far too soon. Your death and the effect it had upon me taught me so much about life. Out of adversity came opportunity, although it took me many years to realise this. Perhaps only now am I grateful for your passion and determination in me to succeed you in business rather than join the Royal Air Force (RAF). I deeply thank you for the foundations you instilled in me - not least of all strength of character.

Following the death of my Father, who was also my business partner (just after my 20th birthday), I stumbled for a short time. The void was quickly replaced by my Father's previous senior partner, Jeff Burgess, who stepped up and became the business role model I then needed. Jeff was driven. He was a man who set high standards of professional conduct and knowledge, and the training and education I received was absolutely first rate. I will always be grateful for the opportunities Jeff provided and his training on all matters to do with investments and capital taxes. He was a fountain of knowledge.

As time passed I grew in confidence and strength. Two colleagues who really encouraged me to move forward were Peter McMullon and Livio Bove. Peter, my manager for a time, was probably one of the funniest individuals you could ever wish to meet. He taught me so much about perseverance and understanding others, the skills needed to become a real 'people person,' a must when you're handling life-changing financial assets. Following Peter, his successor Livio Bove was the one individual who, in all honesty, taught me the most about the craft of my profession. Livio had a management and leadership style that was hugely empowering, and still to this day he remains the same. His belief in me, and the skills he taught me, were a real blessing. Thank you both.

As time progressed, I became more and more fascinated with the psychological elements of human nature and the immense impact goal setting has on realising outcomes.

Paul Armson from *Inspiring Advisers* is a coach for financial planners. Thank you Paul for the impact, input and support you have given me in writing this book and empowering us financial planners!

In June 2003 I set up my own practice and my then soon to be wife Dr. Sarah Pagett (now Lehmann – bless you) unquestionably played the largest part in the subsequent shift I made in my mind and my professional practice. Sarah trained as clinical psychologist and coach, and when I reached a point in my career where I was most definitely bored, she concentrated her coaching skills on me. With ease, she was able to extract the elements of my profession that I was deeply passionate about.

The passion? I wanted to make a difference in people's lives, rather than simply providing financial services. More about that later! So thank you Sarah, from the bottom of my heart, for all the support over the years and your reflecting questions that accompanied me as I wrote this book. Although my writings may not constitute a literary wonder, I do hope the 'pop psychology' and the pragmatic approach I have taken will help people to achieve the outcomes they so desire.

To Harry, Anna and Jacob my three children, thank you for all being patient with me and understanding the demands of my vocation. Hopefully by reading this book, you too will have the skills to live a life of purpose and potential!

And speaking of lives of purpose...Dr. Stephen Sutton M.B.E played a huge part in my writing this book. You only need to search on the Internet "Stephen's Story" to learn more about this amazing teenager and how he touched so many lives.

A local 15-year-old teenager (Stephen) had been diagnosed with cancer and after several treatments was to learn that his cancer was incurable. Despite this devastating news Stephen adopted a positive outlook and set about creating a 'Bucket List' and raising money for the Teenage Cancer Trust (TCT).

I find it amazing and humbling, as faced with this situation one could so easily (and understandably) become depressed, self-focused and simply give up. Not Stephen. He turned his adversity into opportunity and demonstrated a truly remarkable resilience.

I recall talking with Stephen when I was driving him to a speaking engagement, in fact we had many an interesting conversation, and I remember asking how he could be so positive when he was terminally ill. He looked me in the eyes (with that 'Stephen Sutton Effect' that anyone who knew him would know) and said, *"Karl, everyone is terminally ill, they just don't realise it yet."*

With that in mind, I set about writing this book so that other people could 'Design the Life they WANT' - to enjoy everything in earnest and make the most out of opportunities and set backs. To fully realise life and retirement, and to do so with all the sanctuary and freedom they've dreamed of without compromise.

Karl Lehmann pictured with Stephen Sutton of Stephen's Story

To Nickie Brown, the Managing Director of a successful business, who has, through hard work and determination, lived a life of purpose and aligned his decisions with his core values. More about Nickie later and thank you to him for allowing me to tell part of his story.

And finally, I can't help but mention Kay and John. This happy couple are clients of mine who live a life of purpose. They are great advocates and delightful people to work with, so much so that I have dedicated a chapter in the book to them. John and Kay will feature heavily throughout this book as a case study on how to really enjoy life. Thank you for being such willing participants. You're a joy to know.

Thank you all – you've played a part in who I am and what I can now share.

To my wife, Sarah and my three children:

Harry

Anna

Jacob

I deeply love and respect you all.

Let's get started.

INTRODUCTION

What if, in an hour or two, I could share with you a system that would slowly but surely transform your life and your lifestyle?

Then, what if I told you it was a simple proven three-step plan to help you 'Design the Life you Want'? That you could set it up really quickly and that it could all be done from the comfort of your own home, or even lying on the beach? You'd be somewhat interested in what I was going to share. Right?

And what if I also told you this system was called 'Your Financial Life Plan ™' and that after spending just a short time with me, you could plan a life of purpose that meets your values, needs and wants, and you would have greater clarity about the financial tips that will help to support that lifestyle?

And finally, what if I told you it was easy? So easy in fact that once the plan is established you can tweak how your life's direction is changing and keep your finances on track to support those lifestyle choices?

Would I have your attention? I sincerely hope so because why wouldn't you want to prosper in all those ways that deeply mean something to you?

So, now that I've teased your aspiring mind, how would you like to spend an hour or two with me? How would you like to design the life (and lifestyle) you really want (and deserve)?

I hope the facts above have grasped your attention…please do keep reading.

This book has been designed to be read in a short space of time and implemented immediately. It's a really easy read. It's a super easy system. And it's based on common sense, effective coaching techniques and proven financial planning strategies.

> *"I have a plan so cunning you could brush your teeth with it."* **Baldrick, BBC series 'Blackadder'**

Most people have a plan for when they die. A little glum I agree but it's the truth. That plan is called a Last Will and Testament. And these same people don't have a plan for when they are alive! I find this incredible on so many levels. Evidence confirms that if you have a clearly written plan, and share it with someone you trust, then the chances are massively stacked in your favour that you *will* achieve what you set out to do. So why wouldn't anyone and everyone just do this? Even Baldrick had a plan, although I have to point out that my strategies are a little more robust than Baldrick's and will include more than a simple turnip!

WHO WILL PROVIDE FOR YOUR FREEDOM?

It is a fact of life that in the Western countries, such as the United States of America and the United Kingdom, we have a top-heavy population. Put simply this means there are not enough young people paying into the state 'system' with taxes to support the rising ageing generation who need to draw out of the pot. Therefore no government can afford to provide the same level of benefits that, in the past, used to be a given once you reached retirement age. We can see this throughout the state system with healthcare changes and the burden of providing pensions for employees moving from the state to the employee and employer. With that in mind everyone needs to plan more for their financial future. It won't be a given anymore. FACT.

WHO WANTS FUN, FREEDOM AND CHOICE?

Most people, most of the time, aim at nothing and they hit this with tremendous accuracy.

That said I am not talking about living lives of quiet desperation! I'm talking about freedom, choices, abundance, peace of mind, and security. A lifestyle that's defined as yours, a financial freedom plan that works for you.

WHAT YOU SHOULD HAVE BEEN TAUGHT AT SCHOOL... BUT WEREN'T

The purpose of this book is not just to share a few coaching and planning secrets with you. It is to encourage you to put them into practice.

Now let's be clear about something. I'm not promising to 'transform your life and financial position' overnight. This is not a 'get rich quick' book.

And I'm not talking about helping you gain a millionaire's lifestyle in a few weeks, or even a few months. What I will guarantee is that you'll learn how to have a life that is in harmony with who you are. To begin to understand what your values are as a human being and what your beliefs are as a whole. This is going to be a steady ride for most people in many cases, although I have seen some stellar changes in people and their lives. The deciding factor in the equation is you. How much effort you put in and how you engage with the process. This may not sound as exciting as having the ideal life overnight, but trust me, it's more real this way. Like I said before, it's tried and tested and I use this process day in day out with my private and corporate clients.

HOW THIS BOOK WORKS

Firstly, we will reflect on some basic psychology. Then we'll meet Kay and John. These real clients have a very moving story and are really living an amazing lifestyle.

What's incredible is that they have grasped the process with both hands to create a 'Bucket List' and we work together to make their dreams become a reality. In a way I'm their travel agent. I don't book their flights or accommodation in hotels; I effectively work with them to move forward from where they are now to where they want to be. Usually (for them) that involves lots of astounding holidays, some of which we'll experience a little throughout this book.

So, read their story and let it sink into the pools of your mind. It's a powerful message that I promise will change your thinking and your relationship with money. To make sure you're on track and understand the methods I'm sharing with you, after each chapter there will be a short exercise for you to complete to reinforce the meaning.

PLEASE DO MAKE NOTES

The gentleman in the image to the left was a famous German psychologist, Herman Ebbinghaus, who conducted a study on memory AND how we forget information.

In simple terms we forget:

- 60% of what we hear within 60 minutes
- 80% within a month

Therefore I implore you to please, please, please carry out the exercises included at the end of each chapter. They are there for a reason, they really do matter and they really will make a difference.

KEEPING IT SIMPLE

There are many sophisticated wealth management books out there that will tell you all you need to know about money, how to invest, where to invest and how to become a pseudo financial planner. Let me be clear – this book is not one of them!

This book offers a down to earth approach to life and financial planning. This is *NOT* a regulated financial plan. The verified tips and techniques are simply here to help you get more out of your life and your money.

If after reading this book, should you wish to work with a professional planner I have detailed some information on how you can start to select a planner that is right for you.

LIFE IS NOT A REHEARSAL

The following piece was written by an eighty-five-year old man who learned that he had but just a few days to live...

"If I had my life to live over again, I'd try to make more mistakes next time.
I wouldn't be so perfect. I would relax more. I'd limber up.
I'd be sillier than I've been on this trip.
In fact, I know very few things that I would take seriously.
I'd be crazier. I'd be less hygienic.
I'd take more chances.
I'd take more trips, I'd climb more mountains, I'd sail more seas.
I'd swim more rivers, I'd go to more places I've never been to.

I'd eat more ice cream and fewer beans.
I'd have more actual troubles and fewer imaginary ones!
You see, I was one of those people who lived sanely and sensibly hour after hour, day after day, year after year.
Oh, I've had my moments, and if I had it to do over again, I'd have more of those moments – moment by moment by moment.
I've been one of those people who never went anywhere without a thermometer, a hot water bottle, a raincoat and a parachute.
If I had it to do all over again, I'd travel lighter next time.
If I had it to do all over again, I'd start out earlier in the spring and stay away later
in the fall.
I'd ride more merry-go-rounds,
I'd watch more sunrises,
I'd play with more children,
If I had my life to live all over again...
But you see...
I don't."

Jorge Luis Borges

Isn't this a beautiful reminder?

Let me ask a question. What's achievable for you today, tomorrow and the impressive future ahead?

We only have so long on this planet. Let's make the most of it! Let's build a financial freedom plan that works for you.

PART ONE:

EXPLORE YOUR LIFE GOALS AND CURRENT FINANCIAL SITUATION

CHAPTER 1

MASLOW – THE THEORY OF HUMAN MOTIVATION

"Everyday is a chance to be a better person and to do something positive with your life." **Stephen Sutton**

In 1943, a US psychologist Abraham Maslow published a paper called **A Theory of Human Motivation**. His paper outlined a concept that people had five sets of needs and that these needs happened in a particular order. As each level of need is satisfied, the desire to fulfill the next set of needs will subsequently kick in.

While there were no pyramids or triangles in the original paper, Maslow's hierarchy of needs is now usually illustrated with the levels laid out in a triangle.

1. Physiological Needs

First, we have the basic needs for Biological and Physiological fundamentals that allow us to function. Those of air, food, drink, shelter, warmth, sex and sleep.

2. Safety Needs

Then there is the desire to be safe, to have protection from negative elements, to have security, order, law, stability and a freedom from fear.

3. Social Needs

The third stage involves our need for love, friendship and company. These social needs can form companion bonds with friends, family and work colleagues. Romantic relationships develop which involve intimacy, affection and true love. As human beings we actively seek companionship with others.

4. Esteem Needs

The fourth stage centres on social recognition, status and respect. In our working life and social interaction we work hard to accomplish new achievements, to master new challenges in academia and experience. We seek independence and various levels of status or authority, together with a certain prestige, self-respect and respect from those around us.

5. Self-Actualisation

The final stage, represented at the topmost tip of the triangle, Maslow labeled with the psychologists' term "self-actualisation."

This self-actualisation is all about fulfillment and achieving the very goal that you were put on the planet to satisfy.

> *"A musician must make music, an artist must paint, a poet must write, if he is to be ultimately happy. What a man can be, he must be."* **Maslow**

To realise personal potential and self-fulfillment, people seek personal growth through business and life experiences.

You could say that Maslow's concept depicts the levels in a hierarchy and that the need to fulfill our own being is the most significant.

To know that we strive to use our full potential, and although self-fulfillment enriches us more than any other needs, it is rarely discussed or consciously pursued by most.

Maslow's theory can be applied to financial planning and it is essential to address the needs from the ground up. To work on the fundamentals in order to achieve the greatest level of success is a logical process. A manager of mine once said, "If your outgoings exceed your incomings, then your upkeep is your downfall." And there lies the necessity to deal with first things first!

Throughout this book you will have a series of exercises to complete in order to aid your understanding of the processes I'm sharing. More importantly though, these exercises are designed to engage and empower you to achieve your financial freedom. You will need a pen and you can complete the exercises within this very book.

EXERCISE

1. What needs should I address **immediately** in order for me to move forward with my life?

----

2. What needs do I really **aspire to** achieve with my life?

Ask Yourself These Questions

Are you comfortable enough with the amount of money you have? Is it enough?	Yes	No
Are you spending as much time with family and friends as you would like?	Yes	No
Do you come home from your job feeling fulfilled?	Yes	No
Do you have time to participate in things you believe are worthwhile?	Yes	No
If you were laid off from your job, would you see it as an opportunity?	Yes	No

Do you have enough savings to support you through six months of normal living expenses?	Yes	No
When you think about your finances, do you feel peaceful and at ease?	Yes	No
If you were to die in the next few years, would you be comfortable with your legacy or contribution to your family, your community, or the world?	Yes	No
Are all the aspects of your life - your job, your possessions, your relationships, your values - integrated? Do they fit together?	Yes	No

If you answered 'No' to even one of these questions, you are in the right place! Read on.

CHAPTER 2

THE WHEEL OF LIFE

"Never live in the past, but always learn from it."
Anonymous

The wheel of life is a tool that many business and life coaches use to gain a snapshot of how satisfied a person is with their life. The wheel consists of eight areas that reflect separate extents of life. Some individuals may wish to change the categories to imitate their life more closely.

I'd like you to rate your level of satisfaction in the eight areas of your life with zero (centre of the wheel) equating to not satisfied and 10 (outer circumference of the wheel) equating to highly satisfied.

Please pay close attention to these next couple of tips as you work through the areas.

1. Tell the Truth. All progress begins by telling the truth. Don't cheat yourself as this is for your eyes only and will help you assess the areas of your life you really need to focus on.

2. Don't deliberate. This is simply a snapshot, on this day at this time, so do not over think it. Trust your gut instinct when you score the areas.

Ready? Lets go.

Score the areas on the blank template and remember to include all areas no matter how they look on the scale.

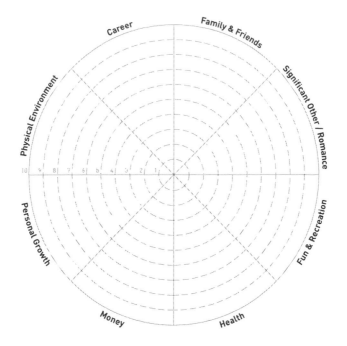

When you have assigned a score in each area the next step is to connect the lines to form an inner wheel. This will indicate an overview of the balance in your life (see the example on the next page).

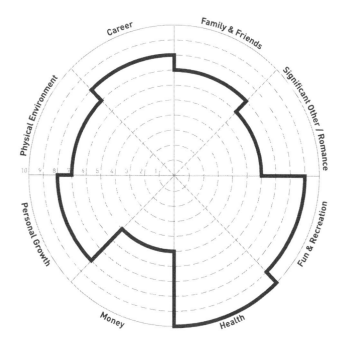

Remember, this is not about getting 10s across all areas (I rarely see that and you wouldn't be reading this book if it was). This exercise is all about creating a smoother ride. Think about it. If this wheel were a tyre on your car, how bumpy would the ride be?

EXERCISE

Now make a list of your results, starting with the lowest score.

Score	Category
1 (Lowest Score)	
2	
3	
4	
5	
6	
7	
8 (Highest Score)	

You have now identified the strongest and weakest areas at this moment in time in your life. The tool will help you to realise where you need to spend more time in order to get your life back on balance. In an ideal world, the wheel would form a relatively smooth circle, which in turn, would coincide with a 'well rounded individual.'

How rounded are you?

Whatever the result, all progress begins by telling the truth.

CHAPTER 3

REAL PEOPLE, REAL LIFE, REAL SUCCESS STORIES

"Wherever you go, go with all your heart" **Confucius**

Throughout this book I will share real life stories with you about actual clients who work with me in my practice. This will hopefully put into context and add real meaning to the tools, tips and techniques I am sharing with you. These are methods that I use on a day-by-day basis with both private clients and corporate executives alike.

In terms of setting the scene, I want to share with you probably one of the most interesting cases that I have had the privilege to work on in a professional capacity.

Back in September 2009, a senior manager of one of the UK's premier Wealth Management organisations introduced a couple called Kay and John to me. The manager concerned used to be their next-door neighbour and wanted a professional financial life planner to work with them. Given the series of events they had recently experienced in their lives, this focus on life planning would be become evident and the reason why it was so critical for them.

When I met with Kay and John we sat down together, and typically, as I would do with any new client, I asked some 'getting to know you' style questions:

1) How can I help you?
2) What is it you are trying to achieve?

What I didn't appreciate was the story that would develop following these two questions.

For the next forty-five minutes to an hour, Kay and John shared with me what I can only describe as one of the most challenging seasons of a person's life that I have heard in my entire experience in the financial planning profession.

In the preceding nineteen months, they had experienced the following:

- May 2008 - Kay had been made redundant
- February 2009 – John's father died
- April 2009 – Kay's mother died
- August 2009 – John was advised of his pending redundancy
- August 2009 – John was diagnosed with Prostate cancer
- December 2009 – Kay was diagnosed with Ovarian cancer

Any one of these events on its own would be a challenging life incident however, to have redundancy, bereavement and life threatening illnesses thrown at you in the space of nineteen months is one heck of a demanding chain of events. Suffice to say, Kay and John were keen to design a life that they wanted to lead and on their terms.

With this in mind we set about implementing the tools and techniques that I use within my financial planning practice to help them identify what some of their core **values** and **beliefs** were, and to then map out the various elements they wanted to achieve in their life.

One film I always recommend to my clients to sit down and watch is *The Bucket List* featuring Morgan Freeman and Jack Nicholson. Corporate billionaire Edward Cole (Nicholson) and working class mechanic Carter Chambers (Freeman) have nothing in common except for their terminal illnesses. While sharing a hospital room together they decide to leave and do all the things they have ever wanted to do before they die according to their bucket list. In the process they heal each other, become unlikely friends, and ultimately find joy in life. There is some great trivia about the film for example, Morgan Freeman's real life son, Alfonso, plays his son in this movie. And Jack Nicholson's own experience in hospital, just prior to filming, inspired some of the dialogue and acting for the movie. The mirrored glasses seen in the film were not originally in the script but Nicholson, who obtained them while in the hospital, brought them to the set and Director Rob Reiner decided to include them in the film for authenticity.

The film can really act as a trigger to stimulate thoughts about what you want to achieve from life. For anybody who has ever lost someone close through cancer, as I have, the first thirty minutes can be quite emotional viewing. Beyond that, there opens an amazing story. The film is a comedy so there any many belly laughs along the way, but there is a real message conveyed and I would encourage everyone to watch it. It will make you stop and think! Not something we always do these days with the pace of life being what it is.

Kay and John set about planning all sorts of adventures. They had an idea that they wanted to learn how to scuba dive (ultimately to depths of 30 metres)! They wanted to travel extensively around the world, to make home improvements and essentially live each day to the full, their belief being that one never knows what is lurking around the corner.

Whilst Kay and John were approaching a young retirement age, the strategies that we use, and that you will learn in this book, are equally relevant to those who are younger in years. If you have your wealth and want to engineer a plan to support the lifestyle you truly desire, this process works superbly well. But equally if, like me, you are in your 'wealth creation' stage, then the tools are even more valuable as you have significantly more time to make sure you have the resources that you need to make a difference.

Nickie is another client I was referred to throughout the course of my business. When I met Nickie, a young managing director of a successful business, I could instantly see he was a very driven, motivated and clear thinking successful businessman. We'll learn more about Nickie shortly but in his case it wasn't travel or money that motivated him. His values were focused very much around his significant other and his family. And to that end he set about redesigning his personal life so that his business life could in fact facilitate all the things that he wanted and dreamt for with regard to those key family values.

As we move through the chapters of this book I will share with you little snippets from Kay, John and Nickie and show you how real people have put these methods and techniques into practice, and how they are achieving the things they have on their bucket list.

Are you ready? Let's continue...

CHAPTER 4

YOUR FINANCIAL LIFE PLAN™ - 'SETTING THE SCENE'

YOU CAN'T STOP TIME!

Fact. No matter who you are or how old you are, precious time is slipping away. So, *WHEN* can *you* start doing what you *really love*?

Living a life of purpose is a commonly used phrase. It often means a variety of different things to different people at different times in their life. To some it can mean being able to enjoy exotic holidays (my clients Kay and John for example), or perhaps being able to own a fast sports car to others. Often it's not even materialist in nature. Living a life of purpose can take on a philanthropic attitude in the act of supporting charities or important causes near and dear to your heart. Often, your purpose can be in providing for the family, working hard to own a stunning home (or second home), a great education for your children, and being able to spend quality time with those you love and cherish (as does Nickie the busy business executive mentioned earlier).

As a father of three, I've always found it quite sobering that children see 'love' and 'time' differently to us as adults. 'Love' in their world means us spending *time* with them. Author John Crudele says that "*Kids spell love T-I-M-E*" and it's a metaphor that I try to consciously remember and make every effort to build into my business life.

When I first met with my client Nickie, it was clear to me that he was a very driven, highly focused young man. He began working as a teenager literally "on the broom" sweeping the factory floor. Now he runs the company. It just goes to show that with the right attitude and a hard working ethic anything can be possible. By the tender age of thirty, Nickie was the Managing Director of a very successful business, which now turns over in excess of £25 million per annum.

When we met, I asked Nickie why he needed my services and his reply went a along the lines of: "Karl, I run a very successful business, I'm very focused on that and working with my team, but there other areas in my life that need planning and you have highlighted those to me. I need to work on the business to get the financial outputs I aspire to, but then I need *you* to make sure my financial plan supports my life plan."

Spending more quality time with his partner and family, buying and developing a family home they were proud of, and private education for his children were key drivers and values that Nickie wanted to provide for and enjoy with his family. They were important to him, but had we not spent the time to find out what was important to him; all the financial discussions in the world would have been worthless and lacking in substance.

Nickie's Family

Nickie's Family Home Developments

These elements are individual lifestyle choices and they are extremely important to us. Shortly, we will explore ways of finding out what is really important to *you*, as we are all different and it's the individual goals that will mean the most. In essence we will capture all of those 'one day I must' moments.

Why Have A Financial Life Plan?

Do you remember earlier when I said most people have a plan for when they are dead, such as a Will that describes what they want after they die, but don't have a plan for when they are alive?

There is plenty of evidence out there that shows that if you have a clearly written plan and share it with someone you trust, then the chances are you *will* achieve it.

And, to add value to my profession, people who follow qualified financial advice have two and a half times the retirement savings of those who have not.[1]

Now I am not talking about leading a life of quiet desperation. I want to empower you to live a life full of passion, purpose and above all, fun. I want you to be able to make a fulfilling contribution in your work place, your home and your community. To make a difference wherever you choose and desire to do so.

Your Financial Life Plan™ is Life Planning combined with Financial Planning.

If money is the means to an end - then what does the end look like to you?

Life(style) Planning helps you to understand what is truly important to you.

The Psychology!

My wife is a clinical psychologist so I write the next paragraphs with a little caution. Let me be clear, this is not a clinician's academic book. This is an explanation of how our values and beliefs shape who we are.

Beliefs

The dictionary definition says a belief is, *"A principle accepted as true or real without proof. An opinion, a conviction."*

Our beliefs are assumptions that we make about the world and everything and everyone in it.

These beliefs grow from what we see, hear, experience, read and think about.

Think back to your childhood. How was your behaviour affected by what someone else said about you? Perhaps a cutting remark from a teacher such as "What a stupid answer!" Would that have made you think twice about raising your hand in class for fear of ridicule and humiliation?

And such a small in-the-moment comment might have affected you for years to come in questioning your understanding and skill. But were you stupid? Probably not. I suspect the teacher was rather lacking in his or her own skills, or maybe they were just simply having a bad day. It is this process of our perception that affects us and how we perceive the things we see, hear, experience and think. The great news is we can challenge those thoughts and ultimately change perception.

Now what I really want to focus on is our values.

Values

These are the things that we deem important:

Equality	Honesty	Education	Effort
Perseverance	Loyalty	Faithfulness	Justice
Freedom	Kindness	Compassion	Determination
Integrity	Joy	Love	Modesty
Open-mindedness	Personal growth	Punctuality	Professionalism
Trust	Eco-conscious	Fair	Optimistic
Passionate	Reliable	Spiritual	Tenacious
Enthusiastic	Hope	Ethical	Humility

Remember Stephen Sutton, the amazing teenager from Stephen's Story we heard about earlier in the book? Well he said, *"The fact that life sometimes doesn't seem fair fuels my motivation to make the world a better place. Bad things happen, but it's how you react to these things that define who you really are."*

Stephen's core values were: -

1. **Help** others
2. **Achieve** something
3. **Enjoy life** – "have a fantastic time" and perhaps above all else
4. **Make A Difference**

Every decision we make is based on our values and we either use them as avoidance or for aspiration.

Clarity

The clearer you can be about your values and beliefs, the happier and more effective you will be in achieving your goals in life. And hence the importance in setting out Your Financial Life Plan™.

EXERCISE

Take a minute or two to list the values you really do hold dear to yourself.

Think about this carefully because they will form the core elements within Your Financial Life Plan™. The three key steps of the plan will include:

1. **EXPLORE** your life goals and your current financial situation

2. **PLAN** your wealth management strategy

3. **REVIEW** your wealth management strategy to keeping it on track

CHAPTER 5

WHAT'S IMPORTANT ABOUT MONEY TO YOU?

"If it is important to you, you will find a way. If not, you'll find an excuse". **Unknown**

Now it's time to consider in depth Your Financial Life Plan™.

STEP 1: EXPLORE

Now we are going to consider a 'values based' questioning exercise, which applies an established coaching methodology.

In a couple of pages ahead, I've included a working template for you to make a note of your answers. That way you'll always have something to refer back to.

1. Ask yourself, "What's important about money to me?" Write your answers in box number 10, capturing the essence of what's important about money to you and use words that are meaningful – hopefully this should be relatively easy.
2. Now, ask yourself, "What's important about **your last answer...** to you?"

I'll give you an example; if your first answer was security then the question now becomes what's important about **security** to you?

The answer might be freedom in which case you'll need to add freedom to the next box and the question is rephrased to what is important about **freedom** to you? In a way you are walking up the values staircase. Just keep going!

3. Repeat this process for 7–10 steps, or when you come to a natural end. **Note** – sometimes it can seem as though you loop around in circles, but persevere with it. This is just because our brains are not always used to thinking in this way!

Your first answer is likely to be about the basic things in life that money delivers. Words/sentences I often hear include "Security," "Freedom," "Time," or "Independence."

As you work through the exercise your responses will move from the basic needs that money fulfills and escalate towards the things that are important to you at a deeper level. Remember Maslow?

When we progress past the initial monetary needs, it will free you to consider other higher values in life. Generally this is often something that is beyond our own needs. People tend to ultimately look outwards, usually at something to do with others.

Answers I often hear in my practice include, "Helping the kids to have great childhood experiences," "Giving back to the community," or "Securing a better future for the planet." This exercise often highlights issues that are important to you such as the environment, charitable causes, children, the community and even world peace!

Remember there is no right or wrong answer. Wherever this goes is fine, it's all about what's important to you.

What's important to you?

1
2
3
4
5
6
7
8
9
10

You will see that the answers at the top of your list are now beginning to form your 'why I'm here.'

Along the staircase you should have some 'ah ha' moments. Remember to capture those too and write them down here. What have your learned about yourself?

'Ah Ha' Moments

CHAPTER 6

GAINING SOME PERSPECTIVE

"If you change the way you look at things, the things you look at change' **Wayne Dyer**

In this chapter I'm going to ask you three simple questions that will encourage you think big, gain perspective and ultimately help you to formulate your central mission in life. There is a helpful template on the next page where you can make a note of your answers.

OK, the first question, "If money was no object, what would you do with your life?" Remember to think really big about this, no holding back now!

The second question brings a little perspective into what really matters to you in life and if you received the crashing news that there wasn't much time left, what would you do differently? Think deep and think hard about this, as it can be difficult when you are hypothetically thinking. Jot your answers down in the template.

And finally the third question, as hard as it is to write down what your biggest regret is, it will certainly help you to focus on what really matters.

By now you should have compiled a series of those 'one day I must' moments.

Now let's plan them out.

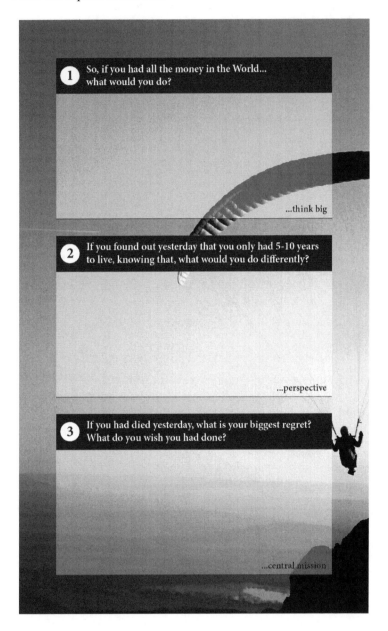

1 So, if you had all the money in the World...
what would you do?

...think big

2 If you found out yesterday that you only had 5-10 years
to live, knowing that, what would you do differently?

...perspective

3 If you had died yesterday, what is your biggest regret?
What do you wish you had done?

...central mission

CHAPTER 7

YOUR PERSONAL MILESTONES

"Vision without action is a day-dream. Action without vision is a nightmare" – **Japanese proverb**

Given your answers to the coaching questions in the previous two chapters, and reflecting on your wheel of life, what are the areas in your life you feel you would like to address sooner rather than later?

These areas can be financial, business, spiritual, family, career, health, charitable, or personal development. In fact, they can be anything that makes you and your life great. Please do have fun with this next part.

What you need to do is capture, on the map at the end of this chapter, all the things that you have identified and want to do, be or have. Then (and this is very important) I need you to put a date next to the area in question for when you want to achieve it.

Essentially what you are concentrating on here is setting your own personal goals that are **S.M.A.R.T.** in purpose.

- **S**pecific
- **M**easurable
- **A**chievable
- **R**esults-focus
- **T**ime-bound

Some people use **S.M.A.R.T.E.R.** with the **E** standing for Exciting and **R** for Rewarding. This can make it more alive and real for you so please choose whatever you feel more comfortable with.

If you're unsure as to what those headings relate to, don't worry, here's a more detailed explanation.

SPECIFIC

What exactly do you want to achieve? The more specific you can be with your description, the bigger the chance you'll get to accomplish your goals.

A bad example is 'I want to be rich.' This is not specific.

A better example would be that I want to have saved **£100,000** in my **Individual Savings Account (ISA)**.

MEASURABLE

Having measurable **targets** means that you identify exactly what it is you will see, hear and feel when you reach your goal. Being measurable requires you to break down your goal into quantifiable elements with concrete, tangible evidence. Being healthier is not evidence. Not smoking anymore because you adhere to a healthy lifestyle is. See the difference?

ACHIEVABLE

Is your goal achievable?

Do you have the time, money or talent to reach a certain goal? If you don't then you will probably fail and be all the more miserable for it. Please bear in mind that you can ask people to work with you on these goals, as it's helpful to acquire the support and the talent of others. You don't have to do this alone. Remember what I said earlier about sharing your plan?

That doesn't mean that you can't take something that may seem impossible and eventually make it happen. You most certainly could do so by planning smartly and going for it!

I have always lived the by adage, "If you shoot for the stars and hit the moon you'll still be happier than never having taken the shot at all."

RESULTS FOCUS

Is reaching your goal relevant to you? Do you really and truly want to run a large business, have a busy job role, be famous, or have three children? How will your life be different and how will you feel having achieved your goal?

Focus on what you really desire and want from your goals and be realistic about what you can control. More about this particular element in just a moment.

TIME

Everybody knows that deadlines are the critical factor in what makes most people take decisive action. Attach deadlines to your goals for you to work towards but keep the timeline realistic and flexible. That way you can also keep your sanity!

Being too stringent can often make objectives seem like a race against time, which is most likely not how you want to achieve anything. From personal experience I found that this could add undue pressure, which in turn can often be very stressful; if you don't achieve something you wish for, it can often make you feel as though you have failed.

Personally I prefer to work on challenging daily 'standards.' This means that if today I underperform, I practice the principle of being kind to myself and not beating myself up about it. Tomorrow is another day that will bring with it another opportunity to succeed.

This way you feel like an achiever on a daily basis, rather than feeling that the goal objective is slipping away. I sometimes found scary goals exactly that, too scary.

I know we are all wired differently and I have many business colleagues who thrive on that pressure! That approach doesn't work for me, and it may not work for you. This is a journey about finding out what honestly works for you. You are unique and you need to trust your 'gut instinct' on how best to manage yourself.

I spent much of my career setting goals for every little detail, analysing it frequently and I actually ended up missing the point (the big picture)! Nowadays I trust myself to know what I need to do on a daily basis and focus on that. Success is hidden in your daily routine. Everything counts and is either moving you closer to, or further away from, where you want to be.

So turning back to Kay and John, here is a great example of a SMART goal.

Kay and John were enjoying the grand Queen Mary 2 ocean liner whilst on a two-week cruise around Norway. They were offered a phenomenal cruise package for October 2013 after which Kay immediately called me from the ship. The deal was typically only valid for that day so goals were needed in order to achieve this dream holiday for Kay and John. See if you can spot the SMART elements they needed...

- To go on a cruise but not just any old cruise (that's vague and not dreaming in Technicolor), they wanted to sail on the Cunard Queen Mary 2, **the largest ocean going liner in the world**
- They wanted to sail transatlantic from Southampton to New York and stay on board to sail up through New England to Canada, taking in a number of stops along the way including Halifax and Quebec. They wanted to return down the Canadian and United States coastline and sail back to England. All in all they would be on board for 27 nights
- Although they originally planned and booked the Princess Grill state room, they were later offered the Queens Grill state room (for an upgrade fee of course) where the provision of a personal butler would provide an awesome passenger experience
- They wanted to do this in October 2013

The only challenge to achieving this goal was whether it was realistic at the time. With Kay chatting on the phone she mentioned the words 'state room,' and claxons went off in the back of my head as to whether this was achievable due to the quantity of money needed in a short space of time. However, Kay and John were determined to achieve this goal and they were able to raise the money needed to fund the trip, with focused effort, and in the required timescale. Therefore this goal became realistic.

And so to recap. Write out the key goals you want to achieve in your life and make them **SMART or SMARTER.**

When you have your SMART goals write them into your Personal Milestones template below, and set yourself stretching/exciting but realistic daily standards of actions you need to take in order to achieve those longer-term goals.

Kay & John having achieved their goal; as dive buddies in the Red Sea.

A future goal – Planning to be on one of the three Cunard Queens for the 200th Anniversary (2040)

Living Life in the Fast Lane (149 mph down the straight) – John driving a NASCAR at Daytona

Your Personal Milestones

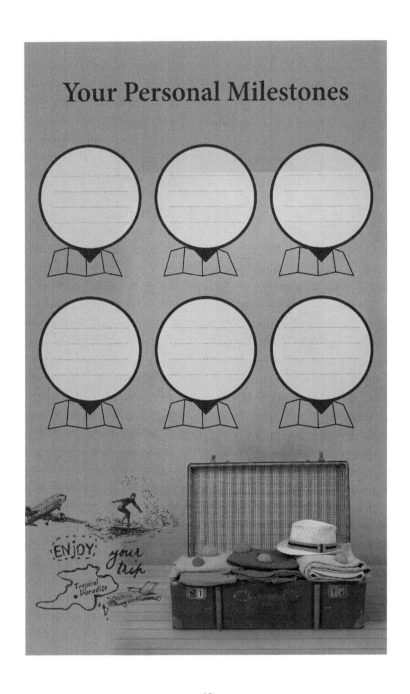

PART TWO:

PLAN YOUR WEALTH MANAGEMENT STRATEGY

CHAPTER 8

TELLING THE TRUTH ABOUT MONEY

"If your outgoings exceed your incomings, then your upkeep is your downfall."

Building appropriate resources around you is an important part to make sure that you feel comfortable and secure.

"Prevention is better than cure" and this applies to the concept of seeking financial planning advice.

STEP 2: PLAN

Taking proactive planning for your future is a sound strategy for preventing financial worry or concerns.

I am not going to delve into too much detail with regards to specific financial planning, as each circumstance will by its nature, be different and call for a different approach. Rather, I would like to give you some common tips and techniques that will help you to tell the truth about your money situation.

INCOME

For most of us, our income is easy to calculate as it may include:

- Your salary if you are employed or your profits/drawings if you are self- employed
- Investment Income i.e. interest or dividends
- State benefits
- Pension income

A useful exercise is to get into the habit of regularly reviewing your bank statements to capture this information. Have a go at completing the tables below.

Income Summary	Name 1		Name 2	
	Taxable	Non-taxable	Taxable	Non-taxable
Employment Earnings				
Self-employed earnings				
Pension Income				
State Pension Income				
Investment Income				
State Benefits				
Income from Other Sources				

Monthly Income Summary

	Name 1	Name 2	Joint
Total Monthly Net Income (after tax)			

EXPENDITURE

Understanding your expenditure can be a little more complicated. By putting time aside in order to understand how you spend your money will often allow enormous benefits to be gained. The process will enable you to see where your money goes and therefore identify where you can best make savings. It may also highlight where you may, unknowingly, be wasting valuable wealth.

Try to get into the habit of keeping a regular log, especially for cash purchases, and try your best to analyse all of your expenditure using your bank and credit card statements. Trust me you will be surprised at what you learn!

The difference between your net income and your expenditure is 'disposable income.' This is the monetary resource that you can actually do something productive with. I always think of money as energy. It allows us to do things, whether good or bad, and helps to fuel our goals and dreams.

Put simply, if you are spending more than you earn then you need to deal with the situation immediately before it gets out of hand. One option could be to try and increase your income, but above all else, learn to reduce your expenditure.

Finally in terms of expenditure, it is useful to think about what that currently entails. Also, if you are looking towards planning for the future i.e. after retirement, try and dream about what your lifestyle will look and feel like. Use the Expenditure Questionnaire overleaf to log your activity.

Name:	Annual Expenditure				
Date:	Now		Future Desired Lifestyle		
	Current lifestyle		At selected retirement		Post Age 75/80
Housekeeping expenses			Note: In today's pounds please!		
Electricity					
Gas					
Water Rates					
Council Tax					
Home Telephone					
Repairs and renewals					
Solid Fuel					
Oil					
Garden/Gardener/Plants etc.					
Help in house					
Home & contents insurance					
Other Insurance					
TV License					
Sky/Digital TV					
Any other expenses					
Alarm					
Internet					
Housekeeping/Food etc.					
Pet foods					
Other private annual expenses					
Total					

Children's expenses					
Childcare/babysitters					
Clothing					
Education expenses					
Pocket-money					
Other Expenses					
Total					

Personal Expenses					
Clothing and footwear					
Cigarettes and Tobacco					
Eating out					
Christmas and Birthday presents					
Holidays					
Subscriptions (e.g. AA/RAC Etc.)					
Sports/Hobbies					
Health Insurance					

Mobile Phones				
CD's/Books/Newspapers				
Other Misc. spending money				
Gifts to charities				
Travelling expenses				
Other personal expenses				
Total				

NET WORTH

After calculating your income and expenditure it's time to work out your net worth position. This is the difference between your assets (what you have to your name) and your liabilities (what you owe to others). Log your assets and liabilities below to gain an overview of your position.

		Current Values
Category		
Land/Buildings		£
Personal Assets		£
Bank/Building Society		£
National Savings		£
Premium Bonds		£
Individual Savings Accounts		£
Shares		£
Bonds		£
Other Investments		£
Life Policies (not in Trust)		£
Pensions		£
Business Interests		£
Total Assets		£
LESS: Liabilities (Loans, credit cards, mortgage etc.)		£
EQUALS: Net Worth		£

Once you have carried out this exercise it is worth pausing to reflect on how your current financial reality is looking.

Whilst it is important to be realistic about your current situation and vision, this is a future lifestyle that you are considering. So plan for the best and think, do you want to enjoy your retirement, or retire from enjoyment?

Are you spending more than you are earning? Do you have surplus income? If so, do you know where it goes?

With regards to your net worth and assets and liabilities, do you own more than you owe?

How much money have you managed to save in the last 10 years? If income isn't allocated it will have been spent.

What are the objectives of your investments? Are you investing for the money to grow or to provide you with an income? Or both?

If you don't have objectives how do you know when you have achieved them? What areas of your finances does the above exercise show you?

CHAPTER 9

SHORT, MEDIUM AND LONGER TERM PLANNING

"Planning is bringing the future into the present, so that you can do something about it now." **Alan Lakein**

The process of short, medium and longer term planning is a huge subject and beyond the scope of this book alone. The following points are designed to be very broad guidelines for your consideration and to assist in deciphering what sort of savings or investment vehicle is the most appropriate for your planning.

THE SHORT TERM BUCKET

In 99.99% of cases this is the first and most important part in any savings and investment plan. Get this part right and everything else will fall into place.

Every person needs a short-term 'emergency fund'. This is a fund whereby you have allocated money to a safe investment and the capital value will **not** fall. Money that is earmarked as your emergency fund should ideally be kept in a **cash deposit** account with a bank, building society or suitable National Savings and Investment account.

The account will probably bear little interest although it must be easily accessible as this is the most important consideration.

The purpose of your short-term emergency fund is precisely that, for emergencies such as car repairs or replacing an essential appliance that has broken. The fund can also be used as a bridge to get you through temporary financial challenges such as a job loss.

When you have an emergency fund, you also have peace of mind. Your money is there, safe secure and readily available. This means you don't have to panic if you need to come up with money quickly nor will you need to turn to credit cards which can be a slippery road. Even if your emergency fund isn't big enough to handle everything, it can still help to reduce the amount of money you must look for from other areas. And it will certainly help to reduce your stress level.

I normally ask my clients, "How much money do you need in reserve to put your head on the pillow at night and sleep easily?" Whatever that figure is, add a little more and you'll be safe in the knowledge that you should be covered in the event of an emergency.

We also need to look at how many months' expenditure you will need to cover should your main income unexpectedly cease. As a general rule (and this depends on age and whether you are working or retired), I would suggest three to six months for young adults but as we age, this figure would generally need to be increased. The ability to earn 'new money' in retirement for example is usually not an option, therefore extra care is needed when allocating assets to the various areas.

The figure should be easy to work out from the exercise completed earlier. The amount you save in an emergency fund is down to individual preference but make sure you're happy with what you set aside and if in doubt, always seek professional advice to run through the figures.

MEDIUM AND LONGER TERM PLANNING

Once you have set aside your emergency fund, any other investments or savings that are for the longer term, i.e. six years or longer, should be invested elsewhere. I must stress that this is only **IF** you are comfortable with the risks that go with longer term financial planning.

Medium and longer-term investment can include collective investments such as unit and investment trusts, Individual Savings Accounts (non-cash account version), Pensions and various forms of Investment Bonds etc.

So why invest in these areas?

Inflation of course. Never overlook the impact that inflation can have on the spending power of your money.

In general, investments that carry little or no risk of falling in value also offer lower potential in return. Thus, whilst the actual value of your investment might not fall, the lower potential return means that over the longer term, it will have a greater chance of being eroded by inflation.

Have you ever heard of the Rule of 72?

Let me explain. If you take the number 72 and divide it by the current rate of inflation, the answer that remains will give you the amount of time (in years) that it would take for your savings or investment to half in 'real terms.'

For example:

72 ÷ 4% = 18 years to halve your investment

An explanation of this rule would be as follows:

- Place a £100,000 investment into your bank account
- Assuming you then spend the interest it earned every year, eighteen years later your bank statement would still show £100,000

However, in real terms, due to the rising costs of living (inflation), your investment would now only be worth £50,000.

In order to combat the effects of inflation you would need to invest in **real assets** otherwise known as investments that will grow and appreciate in value. These real assets include property and stocks and shares.

No investment however is completely risk free. It is down to you to decide how comfortable you are with the prospect of losing money, even if it is a short-term loss before values recover, as you often need to ride the financial market waves when it comes to investments.

Tolerance of risk is different for each of us and it can vary considerably according to our personality, our circumstances and the investment term that we are considering. If you have very little money, never gamble on high-risk investments because you cannot afford to lose it.

If you do invest, remember to spread your investments across a number of different asset classes such as property, equities, corporate bonds and gilts, and investment managers in order to reduce the danger of all your investments falling in value at the same time.

Risks to keep in mind include:

- Your investments falling in value
- Not being able to afford to withstand a fall in value
- Not being able to gain access to your money when you need it. By this I mean money in a bank or building society account (unless fixed for a period of time) is generally easy to access. However if you have money tied up in property it is not an asset that is easy to realise. It can take weeks, months even years sometimes to sell a property.
- The value of your investments not keeping pace with inflation

I stress once again that you should take professional advice on such matters and never enter blindly into this area of investment.

EXERCISE

Consider how much money should you invest in the three areas below in order to achieve your goals whilst allowing for inflation.

SHORT TERM   MEDIUM TERM   LONGER TERM

CHAPTER 10

TOP TIPS – ALWAYS PAY YOURSELF FIRST

"Do not save what is left after spending. Spend what is left after saving." **Warren Buffet**

Reality is that people are living longer. The National Institute on Ageing reports that, although most babies born in 1900 did not live past age 50, life expectancy at birth now exceeds 83 years in Japan.

- There are over 23.2 million people aged 50 years and over, over a third of the total UK population[2].

- There are now more people in the UK aged 60 and above than there are under 18[3].

- The number of people over 85 in the UK is predicted to double in the next 20 years and nearly treble in the next 30[4].

So what does this all mean?

Well, the facts of life are that regardless of political persuasion, our ageing population is having a knock-on effect to our health care system and state pensions. In the UK we see the National Health Service (NHS) struggling to meet the increasing costs of people living longer and the eligible state pension age is increasing.

This means that we now have to live longer before we can draw down on any benefits.

Here's something to get your head around. It is a reality of life that if you do not provide for yourself, **no one else will.**

Think about this for a moment. If you want to live a happy and fulfilling lifestyle, just like Kay and John, then you need to get serious about preparing for this. Providing a nest egg for your future is one of the most valuable lessons you can learn.

Over the years I have read various books and the principle of 'Paying Yourself First' appears in many of them.

What most people do when they get paid is to pay everyone else first, such as the mortgage or rent, household bills, even the taxman. And he is normally at the very front of the queue!

Legally you have to pay your taxes and national insurance and there will be some other necessities but after that, it should be time to put yourself and your family as the priority. Don't get me wrong, this *is* a hard discipline to learn, but one that will make a massive difference in your financial life plan.

How much should you allocate?

I tend to think that 10–15% of your income is a good place to start.

You can create a system to do this automatically by setting up a direct debit or standing order. Better still, try to allocate those savings to be invested into your short, medium and longer-term buckets.

What if you are in debt? Should the strategy be different?

This is a question I get asked often and it's a very good one too. Later in this book I will touch on good debt and bad debt but simply put, if you have a credit card that charges high rates of interest, which many do, it is recommended that you reduce those expensive debts first. Build the emergency fund that I spoke about earlier, preferably at the same time. If you cannot manage this then always reduce the short-term debt first and once you have those plans in place, consider allocating money into your medium term and longer-term savings strategies plus reduci g your longer-term debt such as your mortgage.

In the UK this would tend to be investing your money into Individual Savings Accounts, collective investments that invest in stocks and shares, or pension and retirement planning schemes. Be aware that the accessibility of a pension account is not normally granted until a certain age, whereas in general, ISAs are easily accessible and fairly straightforward. Always seek advice as to which options suit your circumstances better.

One final point to consider is that when I meet with clients and they are investing a sum of money into whatever account, I often ask the question, "Do you feel it?" As you can imagine I usually get a somewhat quizzical look!

When I explain further that what I'm really trying to ascertain is, "Do you feel the pinch when the money goes out of the bank account?" More often than not people say,

"Not really." To which I then reflect back to them, "And bearing that in mind, do you think you will feel the **benefit** of that investment when you then come to utilise the money in the future?" And their response, "Probably not," which often triggers a significant light bulb moment!

EXERCISE

Let's take a look at how much you can realistically save each month.

1. My net income per month is

----

2. The amount I save is

----

3. As a percentage of my net income, that equates to

---%

Take the second figure, divide it by the first figure, then multiply the answer by 100 to get the percentage.

4. I'm just curious. What does your 'percentage' answer tell you about your Financial Life Plan?

CHAPTER 11

TOP TIPS – THE POWER OF COMPOUND GROWTH

"The most powerful force in the universe is compound interest." – **Albert Einstein**

Put time on your side.

Investing isn't just about how much money you have to invest. It's also about how much *time* you have to invest it. And that is due to the power of compound growth.

A simple definition.

Compounding occurs when your earnings are reinvested back into your original investment to continue earning for you. This can often create a snowball effect as the original investment, plus any income earned from that investment, grows together over time. In other words, you gain growth on growth.

The more time allowed for, the more growth potential you have.

Let's just say that you put away £50 every month for 10 years and never invested it or earned any interest on it. After 10 years you would have £6,000 saved. But what if you 'invested' that same £50 every month for 10 years and you earned, as an example 8% per annum on your investment, you would then end up with about £9,150. In this instance you would have gained **50% more** on your initial investment.

The chart below illustrates the power of compounding for different monetary amounts and different growth rates.

Where would you like to be?

Growth of Savings depositing £100 per month

Investing £100 per month into an investment can generate returns as detailed below, depending on the rate of return on your investment. (Note - This ignores any charges)

Interest Rate	10 Years	20 Years	30 Years	40 Years
£100/mo invested at 2.0%	£13,294	£29,529	£49,355	£73,566
£100/mo invested at 3.0%	14,009	32,912	58,419	92,837
£100/mo invested at 4.0%	14,774	36,800	69,636	118,590
£100/mo invested at 5.0%	15,593	41,275	83,583	153,238
£100/mo invested at 6.0%	16,470	49,435	100,954	200,145

£100/mo invested at 7.0%	17,409	52,397	122,709	264,012
£100/mo invested at 8.0%	18,417	59,295	150,030	351,428
£100/mo invested at 9.0%	19,497	67,290	184,447	471,643
£100/mo invested at 10.0%	20,655	76,570	227,933	637,678
£100/mo invested at 11.0%	21,899	87,357	283,023	867,896
£100/mo invested at 12.0%	23,234	99,915	352,991	1,188,242

CHAPTER 12

TOP TIPS – IT'S THE LITTLE THINGS THAT MAKE A DIFFERENCE

"If you are born poor its not your mistake, But if you die poor its your mistake." **Bill Gates**

Whilst writing this book someone I know asked me the following questions:

- How much do you need to invest per year in order to live the life you want?
- Do you think that people who only earn the minimum wage could live the life they want?

Ultimately the answer to this depends on what *you* want.

What I do know is that even for the more modest savers out there it's the little things that make a big difference. Attitude is key.

Take a minimum wage earner for example who has a poor attitude towards life and works packing boxes in a factory. My sense is that with this 'poor' attitude they'll still be packing boxes at retirement age.

Flip it! Change the attitude, change the focus, change the passion and change the desires. Think of my client Nickie who started work 'on the broom' on the factory floor. Remember that by the age of thirty he was the Managing Director of the company? Just luck? I don't think so.

I heard a motivational speaker once say that desire is more important than ability. And he possibly had a very valid point, as Nickie's attitude was very different to the 'victim' mentality I sometimes hear in client meetings where people think the world/the state/their employer/their parents owe them a living. You need to rise above this very restrictive personality trait.

"The future is there for those that invent it." Alan Kay

If you have challenging daily standards and laser-like focus you can achieve anything you want. The question is are you prepared to pay the price? It's at this point where people often fail.

Jim Rohn, an American entrepreneur, author and motivational speaker, was famous for his rags to riches story. He has a famous but simple quote:

"There are two types of pain you will go through in life, the pain of discipline and the pain of regret. Discipline weighs ounces while regret weighs tons."

That said, even us mere mortals with modest incomes can be financially secure.

As a financial planner I often find that people use their money in ways that are not moving them towards their goals. I went into an international coffee house recently for a business meeting and observed the amount of people picking up a cappuccino, latte or some other fancy beverage on their way into work. And it wasn't just the coffee; the drink was often accompanied with a croissant or cake.

When I worked in a city office I was always amazed by the amount of people who would buy a ready-made lunch at a premium price rather than taking the time to prepare their food at home. So let's assume this person spends a conservative £5 per day Monday to Friday. They do this for say four weeks per month i.e. £5 x 5 x 4 = £100 per month.

Assuming this habit starts at the age of twenty-one and we take this through to the age of sixty-seven, I wonder how much money that would equate to if that £5 per day were invested into something that grew by 6% per annum over that working life. Remember the power of compound growth in the previous chapter?

How much do you think it will be?

The answer is £293,831 - almost £300,000!

If you are a couple that is £587,662. Note that this is maintaining the same spend of £5 per week throughout those forty-six years, which of course it wouldn't be, due to the cost of inflation as we've already highlighted. So even if you have modest means, your daily habits can move you closer to or further away from your goals.

Now I'm no killjoy, far from it. And I'm not saying don't ever buy a coffee or a sandwich but I would urge you to think how you spend your money and to make informed choices. I would think that by most people's standards an extra circa. £300,000 would be handy for them at retirement. Wouldn't you agree?

EXERCISE

Let's spend a little time on crunching the numbers on some of those menial purchases that could be so much more meaningful.

How much per week do you spend on coffee and other 'incidentals'?

How much do I spend per week on external breakfast or lunch provision that I could provide from home at a fraction of the cost?

CHAPTER 13

TOP TIPS - POUND COST AVERAGING

"When asked what the stock market will do: It will fluctuate" **J. P. Morgan**

P ound cost averaging is a fancy term that describes how you can build up a capital sum by investing into a particular investment vehicle such as an Individual Savings Account, Pension or Unit Trust on a regular, usually monthly, basis. More often than not it is used with equity-based investments rather than bonds or fixed income assets that tend to be less volatile.

The key point about pound cost averaging is that you invest on a *regular* basis. This means that when prices are high your monthly contribution may buy fewer shares or fund units but that when prices are low, your investment buys more shares or fund units. This continuous drip-feed method of purchasing your investment transpires that the average purchase price paid over any given period is going to be lower than the arithmetical average of the market price.

Pound cost averaging takes the worry out of investment decision-making so that you need not panic when the price falls because you will merely be buying more of your chosen investment. And because you are committing funds on a regular basis you do not need to worry about investing all your savings at the top of the market either.

While pound cost averaging can reduce your risk, it's also a strategy that does benefit from volatile markets. The more the market swings, the greater the benefit to somebody using pound cost averaging.

For example, if the market swings down every other month and on each downturn you buy more shares or units, they would be worth even more on each upturn. In a bear market (defined as when the markets go down), pound cost averaging allows you to build up an investment, poised to benefit from a recovery, without having to worry about trying to work out when the bottom of the market will occur.

The strategy does however mean that you would lose out on the best of the growth in a rising market, which is actually a small price to pay for the added security that pound cost averaging will bring to the investment decision-making.

POSSIBLE OUTCOME OF UNITS BOUGHT WITH A MONTHLY INVESTMENT OF £1000

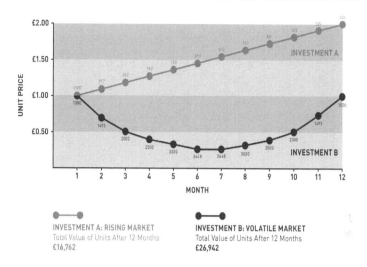

INVESTMENT A: RISING MARKET
Total Value of Units After 12 Months
£16,762

INVESTMENT B: VOLATILE MARKET
Total Value of Units After 12 Months
£26,942

EXERCISE

Do you invest on a monthly basis? If so, how much?

CHAPTER 14

FREEDOM FUND™

"Wealth is not about having a lot of money; it's about having a lot of options." **Chris Rock**

When I work with a client, I try and build a picture of the 'lifestyle' they want to live in the future. We have covered how to "dream it" in part one of this book. Now is the time to "plan it" so that you can really "live it!"

So, the Freedom Fund...what is this all about?

Very simply, it's about posing the question, "How much money do you need in order to make work 'optional'?

If you are working and haven't retired yet, then you need to have some idea of how much money you need in your short, medium and longer-term planning money pots that are going to give you the **lifestyle** you want.

If you are already retired it's more a question of using your capital to produce the lifestyle you would like to lead now.

Financial planners can use sophisticated systems and processes to model the lifestyle you would like and to illustrate any actions you need to take in order to achieve the lifestyle. This will be hard to calculate by yourself, as it can be pretty complex. Tax calculations, inflation assumptions and projections of existing assets need to be carried out, so I would not suggest trying to work out the 'magic number' on your own. That said I hope this book will provide some clarity about what you want your future to look like and where you need to begin.

Calculating your Freedom Fund is an area that requires vey careful planning.

Your key considerations need to include:

1. At what age do you want to make work optional?

----

2. How far away is this in years?

----

3. What assets do you have that will help you in that regard?

----

4. How much do you need in your Freedom Fund™?

Freedom Fund...

MY TOP FIVE VALUES

1

2

3

4

5

FREEDOM FUND...

£

AGE:

EXERCISE

Let's take a few minutes to think about how you currently spend your free time.

1. If you didn't have to work - tell me what you would do?

----

2. Have you had a holiday this year?

----

3. How long were you away?

----

4. Tell me, when you're on holiday, and you have time to spend money, do you generally spend more money than when you were at home or work?

----

5. What are you going to do when you're on holiday for 52 weeks a year? *Reflect on how this lifestyle will be financed.*

CHAPTER 15

WHERE AM I NOW? WHERE DO I NEED TO BE?

"If you are working on something exciting that you really care about, you don't have to be pushed. The vision pulls you." **Steve Jobs**

Essentially there are some key questions in the graphic below that you need to consider in order to work out where you are now and where you need to be.

STEP 3: REVIEW

1. CASH RESERVES

We covered this earlier, but where are you now in terms of your emergency fund? Where do you need to be?

2. GROWTH/INCOME ASSETS

If you are still working, then you are in the accumulation stage of your financial life. Where are you now? Where do you need to be? And are you making progress towards your Freedom Fund™?

If you are already retired, are your investments providing you with the income you really want and need? Is that income tax-efficient?

97

As you progress through the different stages of your life, you will need to review your investments to make sure they are invested in line with your (now) attitude to investment risk.

As you mature in years, what is your 'capacity for loss'?

"Capacity for loss" is a term that refers to considering whether a fall in the value of investments can be absorbed without materially affecting your standard of living.

3. DEBT

"The rich rule over the poor, and the borrower is servant to the lender." **Proverbs 22:7**

Before you borrow money it's worth understanding the difference between good debt and bad debt. Some things are worth going into debt for whereas others can leave you in a rather large financial mess. Here's how to tell the difference.

What is good debt?

In simple terms a good debt is one that is a sensible investment in your financial future that should leave you better off in the long-term and should not have a negative impact on your overall financial position. A mortgage on a house is a great example.

What is bad debt?

Bad debts are those that drain your wealth and are not affordable nor offer any real prospect of 'paying for themselves' in the future. With a plethora of companies trying to lend people money these days, it's an easy trap to fall into. Trust me though, delayed gratification is not only good for the mind, it is also much better for your financial health too. The examples I see of bad debt include:

- A luxury holiday - this can be a trip of a lifetime, but is best avoided if it's accompanied by a lifetime of debt. Instead of getting into debt, try to sensibly save first or take a more modest break in the interim.
- A brand new car you don't need - if you don't need to buy a new car, think twice about it. New cars always lose their value and if you lost your job and couldn't keep up the repayments, you might end up with a loan for more than you could even sell the car for. That means you'd have no car but an outstanding debt (and added interest) to pay.
- Borrowing money to pay the bills and other credit commitments - if you are struggling to reach the end of the month with available funds, then obtain free confidential advice from these website www.stepchange.org, www.capuk.org or www.debtadvicefoundation.org and NOT from someone offering a payday loan!

4. INSURANCE

It wasn't raining the day Noah built the ark!

Insurance is all about the 'what if.' The 'what if you physically fell apart' then at least your financial plan does not need to fall apart with you.

I'm going to ask a series of questions in order to see how you will respond. Remember that I always tell people the truth about money, so I make no apology for the directness of these questions. And there is a purpose to this directness, as I want this exercise to help you to reflect and make positive steps in the area of where you are and where you need to be.

I was just twenty when my father collapsed with a heart attack in front of my very eyes. I performed CPR for twenty minutes until the paramedics arrived but sadly he had already passed. I held my mother's hand when I was thirty as she took her last breath and died from cancer. When you experience such dark events in life, it changes you.

When you lose a breadwinner, you can't replace them, but insurance policies can replace the bread.

1. Is there a history of heart attack or cancer in your family? Or any other critical illness?

----

2. If you had a heart attack, would you rather loose your house or your mortgage?

----

3. If you had been ill for the last six months, how would your finances look now?

Please use the template on the page overleaf to make notes about where you are and where you need to be.

100

WHERE AM I NOW? – WHERE DO I NEED TO BE?

Cash Reserves

Now...

Be...

Debt

Now...

Be...

Growth / Income / Assets

Now...

Be...

Insurance

Now...

Be...

In my professional life I have seen great value in making sure that the appropriate insurances and legal documents such as Wills, Lasting Powers of Attorney, corporate agreements and trusts are in place.

This is a quote from a client: *"Last year we were in the middle of winding up our business with a view to retirement when I was told I urgently needed a heart by-pass operation. The prompt pay out of our critical illness insurance meant that the financial pressures on our company were eased immediately and without it the amount of stress would have been unbelievable. It made a huge difference as we had no financial worries and so I was able to concentrate on my recuperation and return to good health."*

In the event of facing a challenging life event, would you rather be dependent or **in**dependent?

Life insurance, critical illness, income replacement and private medical insurances can help with the impact of acute illness and death within a family. Making sure you are adequately protected in the event of such incidents is crucial to your Financial Life Plan. As ever, I urge you to seek advice sooner rather than later if you have any concerns.

Part three next, let's bring this all together.

PART THREE:

REVIEW YOUR WEALTH MANAGEMENT STRATEGY AND KEEPING IT ON TRACK

CHAPTER 16

MOVING FORWARD

"If you always do what you've always done, you'll always get what you've always got." **Henry Ford**

ffective financial management goes beyond the simple monitoring and directing of day-to-day finances, vital though these are. To build the life you want, both before and after retirement age, and to secure the inheritance you wish to pass on to your next generation, a more strategic approach is essential.

Your Financial Life Plan™ is a comprehensive exploration, planning and review process. This process goes significantly deeper than traditional financial planning advice. At its core is the idea of designing your future rather than simply letting it happen to you.

This process can help you to achieve remarkable results and it is relatively straightforward, consisting of just three simple steps that we have now covered.

1. EXPLORE Your Life Goals and Current Financial Situation

In this part, explore what matters to you and what you want to achieve in your goals, values and aspirations. Look at your current financial situation and the assets, income and other financial resources you'll need in order to realise those goals and aspirations, while remaining true to your values.

Many of my clients say that their initial exploration of this area is one of the most enlightening experiences they've ever had. They say that it brings clarity and a sense of purpose, as values, goals and all those "One day I really must..." thoughts are brought into focus and documented. I hope you experienced some of those moments during this journey.

2. PLAN your wealth management strategy

This is the part where you need to develop a bespoke wealth management plan with financial goals that closely support your life goals.

To get the best outcome you will need a financial planner to help you to implement your plan, to source financial products, to create relevant materials and to provide you with advice and guidance on taxation, managing your assets and other critical areas.

This book should have provided you with some of the tools that will help with structure and to encourage you to begin that journey. I cannot give you the financial planning you will need in this book alone, as people are so diverse and no same approach will be appropriate. I encourage you to find your own 'Karl Lehmann' who is skilled at Life and Financial Planning (see next chapter).

3. REVIEW your wealth management strategy and keeping it on track

Most people spend more time, planning their holidays than they do their lives or their financial plans.

In terms of keeping your plan on track, you will need to review it on a regular basis. You will need to look at the factors such as investment performance, changes in income, assets and life goals, shifting tax rates, and developments in the wider economy. Through regular review and refinement you can guarantee that your plan will perform for you, to ensure that you have the financial resources you need to achieve your life goals.

CHAPTER 17

SOURCING FURTHER FINANCIAL PLANNING SUPPORT

Financial Planning consists of the process of helping you to live the life you WANT without fear of ever running out of money, no matter what happens. The focus is on engineering a financial plan to support your life plan.

Advising on financial products is *NOT* Financial Planning. That is Financial Advice.

Different financial services professionals have various opinions on this subject. I believe advice is what you do (if necessary) AFTER you have carried out your Financial Planning.

Paul Armson, who I mentioned earlier, is a coach for financial planners and I have had the pleasure of working with him for some time. He speaks very clearly about how most people could achieve Financial Independence, Financial Security and REAL Peace of Mind. You could sell everything you own and live in a meagre way in an area of the world renowned for spirituality!

But perhaps this would not be the chosen lifestyle you could become accustomed to after living in the Western world.

In my spare time I attempt to play the guitar. My eldest son Harry doesn't just attempt, he is the lead guitarist in an up-and-coming rock band. Both he and I appreciate the acoustic qualities of certain sound systems.

Some people drive mass-produced midrange cars and never desire to own anything more extravagant, yet I have clients who always choose a premium brand motor for the various luxury embellishments or performance attributes they offer. So just like Harry and I like good quality high-end speakers and some people prefer top quality cars, everyone has their own idea of what desirables are important to them.

Now in comparison my wife wouldn't recognise nor value the difference between a Bose or Harman Kardon system and a 1970's transistor radio! That's what makes us all different and links back to our values as human beings. It's also why, for me, the life plan plays such an important element and offers such a personal journey when it comes to creating a financial plan.

If I refer back to the example above of where I can spend an absolute fortune on a premier sound system yet my wife Sarah sees no value in it, this then could create a certain air of financial tension between us.

To move your life and financial planning forward I do recommend you seek professional, tailored financial help in this regard. This book should be the catalyst to get your thought processes going and get you moving in the right direction.

What next?

So where do you go for professional financial advice?

There are currently two main British Standards, which indicate quality financial advice here in the UK.

CHARTERED OR CERTIFIED FINANCIAL PLANNER

There is the Chartered Financial Planner, which is often heralded as the Gold Standard.

The *certified* mark on the other hand is the only globally recognised mark of excellence in Financial Planning and this is why I chose to become a Certified Financial Planner. It means that I can use the **CFP**^{CM} certification with my name.

That said, many people would feel more comfortable to seek an introduction from someone who is happy to recommend a professional that they already work with.

Please remember, no matter what standard you seek or recommendation you take, ensure that the financial professional you work with is suitably qualified and experienced for the financial planning job you want them to do.

Some questions I would urge you to ask of a new advisor include:

1. What are your qualifications?
2. What experience do you have?
3. What services do you offer?
4. What is your approach to financial planning (i.e. is it financial planning or financial advice)?
5. Will you be the only person working with me?
6. How will I pay for your services?
7. How are you regulated?

8. How often do you review my situation?

And finally, be sure to get the above answers in writing.

If you struggle to find a planner to work with, both the professional bodies in the UK (of which I am a member of and can confidently recommend) will be able to assist you in finding someone that meets your needs.

The Institute of Financial Planning will help you find a **CFP**[CM] like myself, or The Personal Finance Society website will assist you in finding a Chartered Financial Planner.

CHAPTER 18

THE FINAL WORD

Financial Planning consists of the process of helping you to live the life you WANT without fear of ever running out of money, no matter what happens. The focus is on engineering a financial plan to support the dreams and aspirations of your life plan.

I started the journey of writing this book inspired by Stephen Sutton. I'd like to close with an extract of a speech that I found to be especially moving and inspiring.

"Imagine there is a bank account that credits your account each morning with £86,400. It carries over no balance from day to day. Every evening the bank deletes whatever part of the balance you failed to use during the day. What would you do? Draw out every penny, of course!

Each of us has such a bank. Its name is TIME. Every morning, it credits you with 86,400 seconds. Every night it writes off as lost, whatever of this you have failed to invest to a good purpose. It carries over no balance. It allows no over draft. Each day it opens a new account for you. If you fail to use the day's deposits, the loss is yours."

Now, what would you do if you suddenly found yourself with £86,400, or dollars/euros, in your account that disappeared each night, only to reappear the next morning?

You'd take it out and do something with it wouldn't you? You'd give it to someone else, you'd invest it in experiences, people, and things that would last and significantly improve your life and the lives of others.

We are all given the same 86,400 seconds each day and you will never get that time back once it has passed. Stephen's message was to use that time as positively and productively as possible.

Only one life that soon is past, only what's made with love will last.

Bearing that in mind, I wish you all the very best on life's journey.

Have fun!

ABOUT THE AUTHOR

KARL LEHMANN

At the tender age of 17 Karl Lehmann qualified to become one of the youngest authorised financial advisors in the UK. Now with more than thirty years' experience in the profession, and since he joined his late Father as an apprentice, he has achieved Certified Financial Planner status. No mean feat where financial planning is concerned as Karl is one of only 1,000 in the UK who hold the only globally recognised standard of excellence in the field (153,000 in the world).

Through his experience of facilitating many peoples' financial planning needs, and designing the keynote 'Your Financial Life Plan,' Karl introduces a simple yet extremely effective way to think differently and insightfully about your financial plan and the method for designing the life you truly want to lead.

Karl's practice is associated with one of the UK's leading wealth management companies and he passionately guides individuals from all walks of life to plan their future with eager anticipation, not anxiety!

As a qualified business performance coach Karl is well-equipped to support people to fully realise their retirement with all the sanctuary and freedom they've ever dreamt of without compromise.

Life is for living so dream it, plan it and live it!

Here's What They Say About Karl Lehmann

"Karl's "Financial Life Plan" has honestly changed the way in which I look at and invest money in my personal life. His approach around meeting life goals over selling products puts him heads and shoulders above anyone in the market. Thanks to Karl I now have a plan in place so I'll be sunning it on a beach come retirement. Many thanks again Karl."

- Charlie Hutton (Company Director)

"Over the years I've had a number of meetings with Financial Advisors, but I found Karl's approach totally different and refreshing. Karl took time to ask many great questions to understand my personal goals, aspirations and areas of focus, all this prior to discussing any products or financial opportunities. This was a very worthwhile process and really enabled me to clearly define what I was looking to achieve and why, it was great to achieve so much clarity and found it motivational. Once this was completed we could then have a meaningful discussion around options available to support MY goals, MY plans and MY aspirations. Rather than being sold a product or solution, it was very much centred around my personal objectives and plans."

- Martin Hall (Managing Director)

"Karl has offered me great advice regarding planning for the future rather than living for today! Everything is explained at an understandable level, which makes me feel comfortable, and in control. I have recommended Karl to two other clients who feel the same as me."
- Nickie Brown (Managing Director)

"I've known Karl now since 2011, both as a client, a collaborator within a proactive business networking community, and a friend. I hold Karl in very high regard, his intelligence and knowledge of the financial industry is excellent and I would trust him in a heartbeat. Adding to Karl's merits is an extremely amiable and down-to-earth personality. He treats his clients like one of the family, with your best interests in mind at all times. I will soon be building my own Financial Freedom Fund with Karl and I would recommend him to absolutely anyone who needs help with the finances - commercial and personal."
- Anna Woolliscroft (Company Director)

"Karl has provided sound advice to us as we approach retirement age and we have developed great confidence in him through his expert knowledge of his field and his dedication to being at the forefront of new opportunities that have been presented."
- Gordon Hutchinson (Retired)

"I believe (Karl Lehmann) to be a person of integrity, a financial advisor that I feel has his customer's interest at heart, which I have found is not always the case. He has a very good grasp of the financial markets and seeks to broaden this knowledge in the interests of his clients. I have already recommended him to others and would have no hesitation to do so in the future."
- Chester Guillott (Retired)

"I have known Karl and his family as a good friend for many years and more recently as a personal financial advisor. He is clearly most helpful and expert in his advice at all times and provides regular global financial updates re the local and global economy."
- **Dr. John Higginbotham (Retired)**

"Karl has always provided excellent and well considered advice. He is not only well informed but enthusiastic and I would never hesitate in recommending him as a financial advisor."
- **Prof. JDP Whiles-MacConnamara**

"Almost 15 years ago we entrusted Karl Lehmann to the task of organizing our investment and pension needs. He has put so much time and effort into it, to ensure the best possible outcome. We can now take the early retirement, which we had hoped for. Thanks Karl."
- **Mr W. and Mrs V. Sammons (Retired)**

"Karl has always been a careful, considerate and ethical Financial Adviser. Having worked with him for over 8 years now I am very happy to endorse his work and reliability. Clients will be aware that they are in good hands very early on in their relationship with him."
- **Stephen Oliver, The Will Company**

"Karl was recommended to me by a golfing friend who, himself, has used Karl's services successfully. I find Karl to be a pleasant, friendly and professional gentleman who has helped my wife and I put our financial affairs into perspective and we look forward to working with him in the future."
- **Tim Park (Retired)**

"I've known Karl for many years as both a friend and financial planner; Karl has always provided sound, considered advice on all financial matters. I've never had a head for finance, yet Karl manages to make the sea of regulations and associated gobbledygook makes sense."
- **Paul Wilson (IT Engineer)**

"I've known Karl for a good while now and I consider him someone I would totally trust. Karl is a person that I am happy to recommend, as I believe he takes time to get to understand his clients' requirements, their aspirations and helps them achieve and exceed them in a totally respectful manner. Karl is one of the most pro-active people I know, his enthusiasm to a good cause is also testament to the type of person he is."
- **Dave Purkiss (Company Director)**

"Karl has advised me on financial planning matters. Not only have I found his expert advice incredibly useful I have always felt that he puts me as the client first. As with other professional services and trusted advisors choosing a financial advisor can be a very personal decision and you should always feel that an advisor has your best interests at heart. I have always felt this way with Karl and as such would not hesitate to recommend him for anyone who is looking for a financial advisor who puts them first."
- **Philip Oakley (Company Director)**

"Karl has a fantastic knowledge of his business. My wife and I were looking into ways to save for the future. Karl explained to us both in a language that I as a person not familiar with the financial advisory industry could easily understand. He explained the differences of different types of investments in short-term medium term and long-term scenario's. I would highly recommend Karl's services and if you wish to look at various options or have any questions then do get in touch with him. I feel enlightened and safer in the knowledge that we now have security for our family's future."

- Andrew White (Company Director)

"I have known Karl as a friend and colleague and have always found his work to be thorough and of a high standard. Karl strives to do his best at all times for his clients and does so with a friendly and engaging manner. As a professional he seeks to stay ahead of developments within financial services and maintain the highest of qualifications to enable him to be effective in his planning for clients."

- Mark Billage (UK National Director – Christian Charity)

END NOTES

1. BlackRock, Investor Pulse Survey, 2013.
2. Mid-2014 Population Estimates UK Office for National Statistics, 2015
3. Mid-2014 Population Estimates UK Office for National Statistics, 2015
4. National population projections, 2012-based, Office for National Statistics, 2013